Date: 10/20/20

Library of Congress Cataloging-in-Publication Data
Title: Armadillos.
Description: New York: Children's Press, an imprint of Scholastic Inc., 2020. | Series: Wild life LOL! | Includes index. | Audience: Grades 2–3 | Summary: "Introduces the reader to the world of Armadillos"—Provided by publisher.
Identifiers: LCCN 2019027472 | ISBN 9780531129760 (library binding) | ISBN 9780531132630 (paperback)
Subjects: LCSH: Armadillos—Juvenile literature.
Classification: LCC QL737.E23 A76 2020 | DDC 599.3/12—dc23
LC record available at https://lccn.loc.gov/2019027472

Produced by Spooky Cheetah Press

Book Design by Kimberly Shake. Original series design by Anna Tunick Tabachnik.

Contributing Editor and Jokester: Pamela Chanko

Printed in Heshan, China 62

SCHOLASTIC, CHILDREN'S PRESS, WILD LIFE LOL!™, and associated logos are trademarks and/or registered trademarks of Scholastic Inc.

1 2 3 4 5 6 7 8 9 10 R 29 28 27 26 25 24 23 22 21 20

Scholastic Inc., 557 Broadway, New York, NY 10012.

Photographs ©: cover, spine: Joel Sartore/National Geographic Creative; cover and throughout: Astarina/Shutterstock; cover and throughout: pijama61/Getty Images; back cover: Eric Isselee/Minden Pictures; 1: Mark Payne-Gill/Minden Pictures; 3 top: Bianca Lavies/National Geographic/Getty Images; 3 bottom: THEGIFT777/iStockphoto; 4: Nigel Pavitt/awl-images; 5 left: Nowik Sylwia/Shutterstock; 5 right: mamita/Shutterstock; 6: Nicholas Smythe/Science Source/Getty Images; 7 left: Gabriel Rojo/Minden Pictures; 7 right: Pete Oxford/Minden Pictures; 8-9: Berndt Fischer/Getty Images; 10: Julia Christe/age fotostock; 11 left: IrinaK/Shutterstock; 11 right: Heidi and Hans-Juergen Koch/Minden Pictures; 12-13: Gabriel Rojo/Minden Pictures; 14-15: Claus Meyer/Minden Pictures; 16: James Davies/Alamy Images; 17 top left: Victor Suarez Naranjo/Shutterstock; 17 top right: Maryna Pleshkun/Shutterstock; 17 bottom left: Wanida_Sri/Shutterstock; 17 bottom right: Jay Ondreicka/Shutterstock; 18 top: Carl Pearce/Dreamstime; 18 bottom: WorldFoto/Alamy Images; 19 top: Mark Payne-Gill/Minden Pictures; 19 bottom: Bianca Lavies/National Geographic Creative; 20-21: Gunter Ziesler/Getty Images; 22: Bianca Lavies/National Geographic/Getty Images; 23 left: Bianca Lavies/National Geographic/Getty Images; 23 right: Heidi and Hans-Juergen Koch/Minden Pictures; 24-25: Stocktrek Images/National Geographic Creative; 25 bottom right: Zoonar GmbH/Alamy Images; 26 left: Janice and Nolan Braud/Alamy Images; 26 right: Antonio Ribeiro/Gamma-Rapho/Getty Images; 27 left: Kevin Schafer/Getty Images; 27 right: Heidi and Hans-Juergen Koch/Minden Pictures; 28 top: nattanan726/Shutterstock; 28 bottom left: Rolf Nussbaumer/Minden Pictures; 28-29 bottom: Eric Isselee/Shutterstock; 29 top left: Encyclopaedia Britannica/Uig/Shutterstock; 29 right: De Agostini Picture Library/Getty Images; 30 map: Jim McMahon/Mapman ®; 30 inset: James Davies/Alamy Images; 31 top: THEGIFT777/iStockphoto; 31 bottom: Mark Payne-Gill/Minden Pictures; 32: Claus Meyer/Minden Pictures.

TABLE OF CONTENTS

ARMA getting excited to read this!

MEET THE
AMAZING ARMADILLO

Are you ready to be amazed and amused? Keep reading! You'll really dig this book!

What's the big DILL-o?

LOL!
What do you call a flying armadillo? **A SHELL-icopter!**

At a Glance

Where do they live? → Armadillos live on grasslands and in deserts, forests, and wetlands.

What do they do? → Armadillos dig many underground homes. They look for food at night.

What do they eat? → Armadillos mostly eat insects.

What do they look like? → Armadillos have a shell-like covering, short legs, and long claws.

How big are they? →

HINT: It depends on the type of armadillo. Check this out!

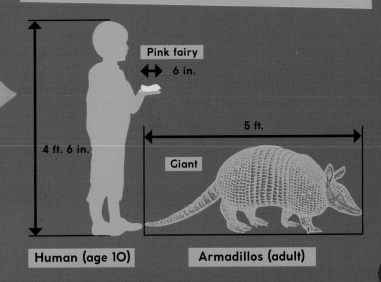

Pink fairy
6 in.

5 ft.

4 ft. 6 in.

Giant

Human (age 10)

Armadillos (adult)

ASSORTED ARMADILLOS

There are about 20 different armadillo **species**. They are not all alike.

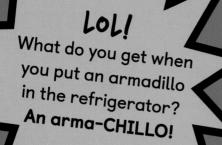

LOL!
What do you get when you put an armadillo in the refrigerator?
An arma-CHILLO!

The smallest armadillo is the pink fairy.

This little critter averages just 6 inches long and weighs only 4 ounces. That's about the size of a hamster.

species: groups into which animals and plants are divided

THAT'S EXTREME!
The giant armadillo's tail is almost as long as three pencils!

They call me mellow yellow.

The biggest armadillo is the giant armadillo.

This animal averages 5 feet long from head to tail. And it weighs 60 to 75 pounds. That's about the size of a golden retriever.

Some armadillos have long snouts.

Other armadillos have short snouts. Armadillos can be different colors, too. They might be gray, brown, pink—or even yellow, like the six-banded armadillo.

FROM SNOUT TO TAIL

There are a few things that all armadillo species have in common.

LOL!
How do armadillos call their friends?
They use their SHELL phones!

Look Sharp
These strong, sharp claws are curved. They help the armadillo dig in the dirt and rip up insect nests.

Tiny Tank

Every armadillo is covered on top by a hard outer shell. Even the top of the animal's face is covered. But its soft belly is unprotected.

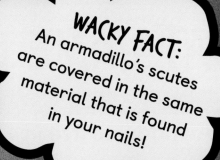

Scute Over!

The shell on an armadillo's back is made of bands of bony plates called scutes. The bands alternate with stretchy skin. That makes the armadillo flexible.

Good Hair Day

An armadillo has hair on its sides and belly. This helps the animal sense the ground while moving around.

AT HOME IN THE AMERICAS

Armadillos live in warm areas. They are found in South America, Central America, and southern North America.

I should have put on sunscreen.

FAST FACT:
The nine-banded armadillo is the only species that lives in the United States.

WACKY FACT:
Armadillos can't live in cold places. They don't have enough body fat to stay warm.

Desert Dwellers

Some armadillos live in desert areas. They include the screaming hairy armadillo. The sandy desert soil is loose and easy to dig through.

habitats: the places where a plant or animal makes its home

Tree House

The giant armadillo lives in many different **habitats**, including forested areas. A home dug under tree roots means a sturdy roof overhead.

Wet and Wild

Some armadillos prefer to live near rivers or streams. The soil is damp and loose there. Believe it or not, armadillos are strong swimmers!

HOT DIGGITY!

All armadillo species have one thing in common—they are experts at digging!

LOL!
Where does an armadillo look things up?
In the DIG-tionary!

WACKY FACT: Armadillos hold their breath as they dig. That keeps dirt from flying into their mouths!

I really dig this spot!

1

Just Right!

Armadillos choose places to live where the digging is easy. They dig to create their homes, called burrows. They also dig tunnels inside the burrows.

WACKY FACT:
Armadillos also dig holes to hide in and to find food.

2
Dynamite Digger

Armadillos use their front claws to dig quickly. They push loose dirt away with their hind legs to keep the area clear.

3
Home, Sweet Home

It takes about 15 minutes for an armadillo to dig a big burrow, which can be 25 feet long. Armadillos will sleep in the burrow up to 18 hours a day.

UNDERGROUND LIVING

Armadillos usually live alone. Each one may have up to a dozen active burrows at a time.

LOL!
What do armadillos eat for lunch?
BURROW-itos!

Room to Spare
An armadillo's burrow may have several different living areas. They are connected by tunnels. Each burrow has lots of openings for quick entry and escape.

No Trespassing

An armadillo marks the area around its burrow. It uses urine and a strong odor produced by scent **glands** on its backside. These markings warn other animals to stay away.

WACKY FACT:
In very cold weather, a group of armadillos may share a burrow to keep warm.

Starting Over

Armadillos don't get too attached to their homes. If food becomes hard to find, the armadillo will move to a new area and start over.

glands: organs in the body that make or release natural chemicals

SLURP IT UP!

An armadillo's diet is mostly made up of insects, insect larvae, eggs, and small animals. Occasionally, armadillos also eat fruit.

THAT'S EXTREME!
One armadillo can eat 40,000 ants in a single meal!

LOL!
What did the armadillo say to the waiter? **The food here is excell-ANT!**

I hope my lunch isn't BUG-ging you!

ants

earthworms

These are some of an armadillo's favorite foods.

spiders

salamanders

TRICKY DEFENSE

Armadillos have many ways to protect themselves from **predators.**

FAST FACT:
Coyotes, alligators, and jaguars are some animals that may hunt armadillos.

Can't Catch Me

When armadillos sense danger, they try to run to a burrow. They run in a zigzag pattern, which makes them hard to catch. Most armadillo species can run up to 30 miles per hour.

Bottoms Up!

The pichi armadillo can quickly dig a shallow hole and hide its face inside. Its shell-covered backside is hard for a predator to grab.

predators: animals that hunt other animals for food

On a Roll

Only three-banded armadillos use this trick! The armadillo quickly folds its body into a ball. Then it tucks in its head, legs, and tail.

SURPRISE!

Up and Out!

A nine-banded armadillo can jump several feet in the air. This surprises the predator and gives the armadillo time to run away.

STARTING A FAMILY

An armadillo is ready to start a family when it is about one year old. Here's one way that happens.

THAT'S EXTREME!
Armadillos can delay giving birth for several months if too little food is available. The female waits until there is enough food for herself and her babies.

Hmm . . . should I give this guy a kick or a wag?

1

Sniffing Things Out

When a male nine-banded armadillo is ready to **mate**, he looks for a female. He sniffs her and waits for her response.

mate: to join together to have babies

WACKY FACT:
A female armadillo hops backward into her burrow to give birth.

female

male

2
Getting the Message

If the female isn't interested in the male, she may kick at him until he leaves her alone. If the female is interested, she wags her tail. Then the two animals will mate.

3
Ready for Babies

The male and female don't stay together. After two to five months, the female prepares a special birthing burrow. This is where she will have her babies.

BABY DAYS

Babies are called pups. There are one to 12 pups in a **litter**. Nine-banded armadillos have four identical pups.

WACKY FACT: It takes from a few days to a couple of weeks for the pups' shells to harden.

LOL! How do armadillos text each other? **They use their SHELL phones!**

I'm king of the mountain!

1

Little Softies

All newborn armadillo pups look like mini adults. But they don't have hard shells. Their skin is gray, soft, and leathery.

litter: a group of animals born at the same time to one mother

2

3

Mommy's Milk

Like all mammals, armadillo pups drink milk from their mother. When they're about two months old, pups begin to eat insects. They still drink milk, too.

We Can Do It!

The pups learn from their mother how to find food and what to eat. By four or five months, they stop drinking milk. They get all their own food.

ANCIENT ARMADILLOS

Huge mammals called glyptodonts are the armadillo's ancient **ancestors**.

THAT'S EXTREME! A glyptodont could weigh as much as two horses!

Supersized
These massive animals lived millions of years ago. The largest glyptodonts weighed about 4,400 pounds. Each was the size of a big car!

ancestors: family members who lived long ago

24

One Tough Customer

A glyptodont had a tough shell. It was covered with bony plates that were 2 inches thick. It also had a club-like tail.

Shelling Out

Some scientists think glyptodonts were wiped out by humans. People hunted them for their shells, which were large enough to use for homes.

Hey there, junior.

Wow. Now *that's* a big DILL-o.

ARMADILLOS AND PEOPLE

We have a long history together!

1800s

Nine-banded armadillos arrived in the United States. Scientists say they swam across the Rio Grande from Mexico to southern Texas!

Mid- to Late 1900s

As more land got developed for ranching and farming, several species lost their habitat. Giant armadillos became vulnerable to **extinction**.

extinction: when no member of a species is left alive

A researcher studies a giant armadillo as it sleeps.

Happy to help!

2011

Scientists in Brazil created new programs to study and protect armadillos. The South American project ultimately reached around the world.

Today

Researchers use armadillos to learn about a disease called leprosy. They are working to develop a **vaccine** to keep people from getting sick.

vaccine: a substance that can protect someone from a disease

Armadillo Cousins

Sloths and anteaters are the armadillo's closest living relatives.

We have long claws, like armadillos do. But we use them to hang from tree branches.

sloths

I feel so CLAWS to you guys.

Please note: Animals are not shown to scale.

Megatheriums

I was a pretty big deal in my day—about 2 million years ago. In fact, I was as big as an elephant.

We were a type of glyptodont.

Doedicurus

anteaters

I'm really good at catching food with my tongue!

The Wild Life

Look at this map of the world. The areas in red show where armadillos live today: Central America and parts of North and South America. Even though armadillos still live in the places where they have always been found, several species are at risk. We want armadillos to continue having habitats to live in.

North America

Central America

South America

What Can You Do?

Groups like the Giant Armadillo Conservation Program are working to keep armadillos—and their habitats—safe! Groups like this one often receive money and support from zoos and from other wildlife organizations.

Ask your parent or caregiver to help you research armadillo conservation groups online. Then think of fun ways to raise money and awareness for these amazing animals.

You could host a car wash or a bake sale and donate the money to your favorite conservation group. You can even adopt an armadillo through the National Wildlife Federation.

Help keep the ball rolling!

INDEX

ABOUT THIS BOOK

This book is a laugh-out-loud early-grade adaptation of *Armadillos* by Susan Knopf. *Armadillos* was originally published by Scholastic as part of its Nature's Children series in 2020.

ARMA see you soon!